CW01090709

# ADRIENNE RICH

*Selected Poems*

1950 - 1995

SALMON POETRY

Published in 1996 by
Salmon Publishing Ltd,
Knockeven, Cliffs of Moher, Co. Clare, Ireland

These poems are reprinted with the permission of
W. W. Norton & Company, Inc., New York.
Not for sale outside the Republic of Ireland and Northern Ireland.

Salmon Publishing greatly appreciates the co-operation and courtesy of
Jeannie Luciano and Naomi H. Wittes of W. W. Norton & Company.

Salmon Publishing gratefully acknowledges the
financial assistance of the Arts Council.

The moral right of the author has been asserted.
A catalogue record for this book is available from the British Library.

ISBN 1 897648 67 7 (Softcover)
ISBN 1 897648 78 2 (Hardcover)

Cover photograph by Mike O'Toole
Cover design by Brenda Dermody of Estresso
Set by Siobhán Hutson in Palatino
Printed by Colour Books, Baldoyle Industrial Estate, Dublin 13

# CONTENTS

# Introduction

When I first read these poems I was in my early thirties. I was married with small children. I was far away from some of the claimed ground here and not yet sure of my own. These are, after all, American poems, written from the heart of the American empire as the century darkens. They are fiercely questioning, deeply political, continuously subversive. They celebrate the lives of women and the sexual and comradely love between them. They contest the structure of the poetic tradition. They interrogate language itself. In all of this, they describe a struggle and record a moment which was not my struggle and would never be my moment. Nor my country, nor my companionship. Nor even my aesthetic.

And yet these poems came to the very edge of the rooms I worked in, dreamed in, listened for a child's cry in. They passed through the frost of a suburban dark, the early light of a neighbourhood summer. I took whichever book they were happening in from place to place, propping it against jars and leaving it after me on chairs and beside coffee cups. Even as I did so, I felt that the life I lived was not the one these poems commended. It was too far from the tumult, too deep in the past. And yet these poems helped me live it.

And as they permeated the small barriers of place and distraction, these poems also began to open my mind to new ideas of who writes a poem and why. A truly important poet changes two things and never one without the other: the interior of the poem and external perceptions of the identity of the poet. By so doing, they prove that the two are inextricable. That these radicalisms not only connect, they actually have their source in each other. After the poem is changed in front of us, after our conservatisms are unwritten by a marvellous cadence or a surprising leap from stanza to stanza, only then do we look up, suddenly ready to see that only someone with a new sense of the poet's life and authority could have done this. But if these poems achieve – and I believe they do – this degree of innovation, they are also rooted deep in a human life. And that perhaps is the place to begin.

∞ ∞ ∞

Adrienne Rich was born in Baltimore, Maryland in the early summer of 1929. Her father was a pathologist at Johns Hopkins University and Jewish. Her mother was Southern and Gentile. One of the poems in this book, 'At the Jewish New Year', states *'Whatever we strain to forget/Our memory must be long'*. Her background was never entirely cast off. On the contrary, the tension between male and female, between historic pride and vulnerable identity has become one of the charged centres of her work.

In 1951 she graduated from Radcliffe College. Within eight years she had received a Guggenheim Fellowship, published two volumes of poetry, had married and given birth to three sons. Somewhere in the middle of all this, we get a glimpse of her one rainy night in Massachusetts, a poignant eyewitness account:

'Short black hair, great sparking black eyes and a tulip-red umbrella: honest, frank, forthright and even opinionated'. Sylvia Plath's first impression of Adrienne Rich, recorded in this sentence in her journals, marks a first meeting. The year was 1958. Adrienne Rich was twenty-nine. The comment catches a woman who was still young, still not quite free of her moorings.

In one sense, how could she be? The American mid-century was an exciting place for a young woman poet to be, provided she looked, and continued to look, as if she would cause no trouble. An example is W. H. Auden's selection of her first volume *A Change of World* for the Yale Younger Poets Award. What the selection gave with one hand, the citation took away with the other. In an odd choice of words, he assigned to the poems little more than the virtues of a Victorian childhood. 'The poems a reader will encounter in this book,' he wrote in his preface 'are neatly and modestly dressed, speak quietly but do not mumble, respect their elders but are not cowed by them and do not tell fibs'. Albert Gelpi, who with Barbara Charlesworth Gelpi, has edited the wonderful Norton Critical edition on Rich's work, says of this comment: 'In other words the stereotype – prim, fussy, schoolmarmish – that has corseted and strait-laced women poets into "poetesses" whom men could deprecate with admiration'.

Adrienne Rich's first two books *A Change of World*, published in 1951, and *The Diamond Cutters and Other Poems* from 1955 are represented by only a few poems here. These are elegantly crafted: the voice is distinct but muted. In one of them, 'Storm Warnings', she writes, *'These are the things that we have learned to do/Who live in troubled regions'*. But a real storm warning does not occur until her third book, *Snapshots of a Daughter-in-Law: Poems 1954-1962*, whose title poem is included here. It is a threshold poem. Suddenly the lines are longer. The voice is clear, fractious and definite: *'A thinking woman sleeps with monsters'*. Here for the first time we catch sight of the mid-century heroine: A woman who shaves her legs until they gleam *'like petrified mammoth-tusk'*, who imagines Emily Dickinson in her Amherst parlour *'while the jellies boil and scum'*. For the first time, we hear a distinctive note: the sound of a silenced woman suddenly able to voice a conventional suppression in terms of an imaginative one.

The poem was a breakthrough. 'It was an extraordinary relief to write that poem,' states Rich in her essay 'When We Dead Awaken'. The early containment of images and line lengths was now over. 'In those years,' she wrote in the same essay, formalism was part of the strategy – like asbestos gloves it allowed me to handle materials I couldn't pick up barehanded'.

From this point the work changed, deepened, strengthened. Between 1964 to 1971 Rich published three books: *Necessities of Life: Poems 1962-1965; Leaflets: Poems 1965-1968; The Will to Change: Poems 1968-1970*. Each is represented in this book. The themes were various, but the signal was clear. The poems would not stay on the page. They were out in the world. They were deep in negotiation with the political climate of the day mediated through Rich's changing sense of her life and the

American ethos.

During these years she moved to New York city with her family. She began to teach in open admissions at City College New York. She was active against the Vietnam War and increasingly involved in the woman's movement. Her father died. Her husband died. By 1974 when *Diving into the Wreck* – a cornerstone volume – was published, she had made a powerful and seamless integration of her lives as mother, lesbian, activist and poet.

Many of the poems that mark this growth are available here. 'Orion' from *Leaflets* for instance, with its glittering, androgynous prince of the night sky, who may well lend some of his elemental grace and endurance to the mysterious swimmer of *Diving into the Wreck*. And 'Planetarium', where the emphasis is not on discovery, but the discoverer: a woman astronomer, opening up the nature of the skies through the nature of her body.

These poems established a forward movement which was continued in *The Dream of a Common Language* (1978); *A Wild Patience Has Taken Me This Far* (1981); *Your Native Land, Your Life* (1986); and *Time's Power* (1989). These, in turn, were followed by the important volume *An Atlas of the Difficult World* (1991) and the lovely, overcast lyricism of her most recent book *Dark Fields of the Republic*.

Space allows only a few signposts. Nevertheless, 'Power', 'North American Time', 'For Memory' and Section XIII of 'An Atlas of the Difficult World' as well as 'Diving into the Wreck' itself and 'Six Narratives' are essential reading. These, with the beautiful love poem which is section XII of 'Twenty-one Love Poems' from *The Dream of a Common Language*, show the extent of the terrain in these poems: a horizon levelled over the political and private lands of an adventurous spirit.

> *I came to explore the wreck*
> *The words are purposes.*
> *The words are maps.*
> *I come to see the damage that was done*
> *and the treasures that prevail.*

∞ ∞ ∞

When the reader finishes these poems and closes this book, one question may well occur. What exactly happened in the tumultuous distance between *A Change of World* and *Dark Fields of the Republic*? What transformed the young poet Auden singled out for her good manners into one of the truly subversive poets of our time? The customary, and sometimes hostile, critical view is that Adrienne Rich became feminist, activist, lesbian. That her angers cut her adrift from mainstream poetry. That America lost a gifted lyric poet and had to make do with a polemicist.

Sexual choice and political disaffection are certainly central themes in this work. But they are ways of attaching this poet to the world, not repudiating it. The love between women, sexual and ethical, becomes a beautiful strategy for imagining a new America, a new order, a different language. It is the irreducible force behind the revelations of love and insistence which energise these poems. Even when that involves – as the line from *Twenty-one Love Poems* suggests – *'all the time nursing, measuring that wound'*.

But Adrienne Rich is also a sophisticated, pilgrim-like traveller in the poetic past as well as the historic one. And in that past, poetry has also been wounded. The fragmentation which she most addresses in her work occurs wherever the moral voice divides from the imagining intelligence.

A number of poems here – 'Diving into the Wreck' and 'Power' and 'North American Time' and 'For Memory' to name just a few – speak to the injustices of a society. They also, and this is crucial, speak directly to that invitation to the poet to remain in a private kingdom of music and perception. Whether flying over the speckled light of New York after dark or fathoming a metaphoric underworld, the inference of these poems is the same: any menace to human beings constitutes a moral imperative, not just for other men and women, but for poetry itself. It is a powerful and essential argument: that the ethical vision is a functioning part of the poetic imagination and not an optional addition. For her discovery and command of that vision at the margins, for her insistence on restoring it to the poetic centre, Adrienne Rich will be seen as one of the shape-makers of this century's poetry.

∞ ∞ ∞

I want to finish with a few sentences from the introduction I did not write here:  the document of

Adrienne Rich's influence on me. Women poets have asserted their place in poetry now for several generations. There are now more poems and more poets. The silence is filling up with words. And so there is coming to be, I believe, an erotics of tradition, in which women will not only influence what is handed on, but how it is handed on. Therefore, the old codes of example and inheritance, the stern bequeathing of poetic authority – which was once presented as the only way to make a canon – is beginning to change. I like to think that the customs of friendship, as well as the loving esteem, which are so visible in the communal life of women, will become evident in the practise and concept of the poetic tradition also. That women poets, from generation to generation, will befriend one another. In that sense I have had Adrienne Rich's friendship. And I could not have done without it.

*Eavan Boland*
Dundrum 1996

*from*

*A CHANGE OF WORLD*

(1951)

# STORM WARNINGS

The glass has been falling all the afternoon,
And knowing better than the instrument
What winds are walking overhead, what zone
Of grey unrest is moving across the land,
I leave the book upon a pillowed chair
And walk from window to closed window, watching
Boughs strain against the sky

And think again, as often when the air
Moves inward toward a silent core of waiting,
How with a single purpose time has travelled
By secret currents of the undiscerned
Into this polar realm.  Weather abroad
And weather in the heart alike come on
Regardless of prediction.

Between foreseeing and averting change
Lies all the mastery of elements
Which clocks and weatherglasses cannot alter.
Time in the hand is not control of time,
Nor shattered fragments of an instrument
A proof against the wind; the wind will rise,
We can only close the shutters.

I draw the curtains as the sky goes black
And set a match to candles sheathed in glass
Against the keyhole draught, the insistent whine
Of weather through the unsealed aperture.

This is our sole defense against the season;
These are the things that we have learned to do
Who live in troubled regions.

# BY NO MEANS NATIVE

'Yonder,' they told him, 'things are not the same.'
He found it understated when he came.
His tongue, in hopes to find itself at home,
Caught up the twist of every idiom.
He learned the accent and the turn of phrase,
Studied like Latin texts the local ways.
He tasted till his palate knew their shape
The country's proudest bean, its master grape.
He never talked of fields remembered green,
Or seasons in his land of origin.

And still he felt there lay a bridgeless space
Between himself and natives of the place.
Their laughter came when his had long abated;
He struggled in allusions never stated.
The truth at last cried out to be confessed:
He must remain eternally a guest,
Never to wear the birthmark of their ways.
He could be studying native all his days
And die a kind of minor alien still.
He might deceive himself by force of will,
Feel all the sentiments and give the sign,
Yet never overstep that tenuous line.

What else then?  Wear the old identity,
The mark of other birth, and when you die,
Die as an exile? it has done for some.
Others surrender, book their passage home,

Only to seek their exile soon again,
No greater strangers than their countrymen.
Yet man will have his bondage to some place;
If not, he seeks an Order, or a race.
Some join the Masons, some embrace the Church,
And if they do, it does not matter much.

As for himself, he joined the band of those
Who pick their fruit no matter where it grows,
And learn to like it sweet or like it sour
Depending on the orchard or the hour.
By no means native, yet somewhat in love
With things a native is enamoured of –
Except the sense of being held and owned
By one ancestral patch of local ground.

# THE RAIN OF BLOOD

In that dark year an angry rain came down
Blood-red upon the hot stones of the town.
Beneath the pelting of that liquid drought
No garden stood, no shattered stalk could sprout,
As from a sunless sky all day it rained
And men came in from streets of terror stained
With that unnatural ichor.  Under night
Impatient lovers did not quench the light,
But listening heard above each other's breath
That sound the dying heard in rooms of death.
Each loudly asked abroad, and none dared tell
What omen in that burning torrent fell.
And all night long we lay, while overhead
The drops rained down as if the heavens bled;
And every dawn we woke to hear the sound,
And all men knew that they could stanch the wound,
But each looked out and cursed the stricken town,
The guilty roofs on which the rain came down.

*from*

*THE DIAMOND CUTTERS*

(1955)

# THE MIDDLE-AGED

Their faces, safe as an interior
Of Holland tiles and Oriental carpet,
Where the fruit-bowl, always filled, stood in a light
Of placid afternoon – their voices' measure,
Their figures moving in the Sunday garden
To lay the tea outdoors or trim the borders,
Afflicted, haunted us. For to be young
Was always to live in other peoples' houses
Whose peace, if we sought it, had been made by others,
Was ours at second-hand and not for long.
The custom of the house, not ours, the sun
Fading the silver-blue Fortuny curtains,
The reminiscence of a Christmas party
Of fourteen years ago – all memory,
Signs of possession and of being possessed,
We tasted, tense with envy. They were so kind,
Would have given us anything; the bowl of fruit
Was filled for us, there was a room upstairs
We must call ours: but twenty years of living
They could not give. Nor did they ever speak
Of the coarse stain on that polished balustrade,
The crack in the study window, or the letters
Locked in a drawer and the key destroyed.
All to be understood by us, returning
Late, in our own time – how that peace was made,
Upon what terms, with how much left unsaid.

# THE TOURIST AND THE TOWN

*(San Miniato al Monte)*


Those clarities detached us, gave us form,
Made us like architecture. Now no more
Bemused by local mist, our edges blurred,
We knew where we began and ended. There
We were the campanile and the dome,
Alive and separate in that bell-struck air,
Climate whose light reformed our random line,
Edged our intent and sharpened our desire.

Could it be always so: a week of sunlight,
Walks with a guidebook, picking out our way
Through verbs and ruins, yet finding after all
The promised vista, once! – The light has changed
Before we can make it ours. We have no choice:
We are only tourists under that blue sky,
Reading the posters on the station wall:
*Come, take a walking-trip through happiness.*

There is a mystery that floats between
The tourist and the town. Imagination
Estranges it from her. She need not suffer
Or die here. It is none of her affair,
Its calm heroic vistas make no claim.
Her bargains with disaster have been sealed
In another country. Here she goes untouched,
And this is alienation. Only sometimes

In certain towns she opens certain letters
Forwarded on from bitter origins,
That send her walking, sick and haunted, through
Mysterious and ordinary streets
That are no more than streets to walk and walk –
And then the tourist and the town are one.

To work and suffer is to be at home.
All else is scenery: the Rathaus fountain,
The skaters in the sunset on the lake
At Salzburg, or, emerging after snow,
The singular clear stars at Castellane.
To work and suffer is to come to know
The angles of a room, light in a square,
As convalescents know the face of one
Who has watched beside them. Yours now, every street,
The noonday swarm across the bridge, the bells
Bruising the air above the crowded roofs,
The avenue of chestnut-trees, the road
To the post-office. Once upon a time
All these for you were fiction. Now, made free
You live among them. Your breath is on this air,
And you are theirs and of their mystery.

*from*

*SNAPSHOTS OF A*

*DAUGHTER-IN-LAW*

(1963)

# SNAPSHOTS OF A DAUGHTER-IN-LAW

## 1.

You, once a belle in Shreveport,
with henna-coloured hair, skin like a peachbud,
still have your dresses copied from that time,
and play a Chopin prelude
called by Cortot: *'Delicious recollections*
*float like perfume through the memory.'*

Your mind now, mouldering like wedding-cake,
heavy with useless experience, rich
with suspicion, rumour, fantasy,
crumbling to pieces under the knife-edge
of mere fact. In the prime of your life.

Nervy, glowering, your daughter
wipes the teaspoons, grows another way.

## 2.

Banging the coffee-pot into the sink
she hears the angels chiding, and looks out
past the raked gardens to the sloppy sky.
Only a week since They said: *Have no patience.*

The next time it was: *Be insatiable.*
Then: *Save yourself; others you cannot save.*
Sometimes she's let the tapstream scald her arm,
a match burn to her thumbnail,

or held her hand above the kettle's snout
right in the woolly steam. They are probably angels,
since nothing hurts her any more, except
each morning's grit blowing into her eyes.

3.


A thinking woman sleeps with monsters.
The beak that grips her, she becomes. And Nature,
that sprung-lidded, still commodious
steamer-trunk of *tempora* and *mores*
gets stuffed with it all:     the mildewed orange-flowers,
the female pills, the terrible breasts
of Boadicea beneath flat foxes' heads and orchids.

Two handsome women, gripped in argument,
each proud, acute, subtle, I hear scream
across the cut glass and majolica
like Furies cornered from their prey:
The argument *ad feminam*, all the old knives
that have rusted in my back, I drive in yours,
*ma semblable, ma soeur!*

4.


Knowing themselves too well in one another:
their gifts no pure fruition, but a thorn,
the prick filed sharp against a hint of scorn . . .
Reading while waiting
for the iron to heat,
writing, *My Life had stood – a Loaded Gun –*

in that Amherst pantry while the jellies boil and scum,
or, more often,
iron-eyed and beaked and purposed as a bird,
dusting everything on the whatnot every day of life.

5.

*Dulce ridens, dulce loquens,*
she shaves her legs until they gleam
like petrified mammoth-tusk.

6.

When to her lute Corinna sings
neither words nor music are her own;
only the long hair dipping
over her cheek, only the song
of silk against her knees
and these
adjusted in reflections of an eye.

Poised, trembling and unsatisfied, before
an unlocked door, that cage of cages,
tell us, you bird, you tragical machine –
is this *fertilisante douleur?* Pinned down
by love, for you the only natural action,
are you edged more keen
to prise the secrets of the vault? has Nature shown
her household books to you, daughter-in-law,
that her sons never saw?

7.

*'To have in this uncertain world some stay*
*which cannot be undermined, is*
*of the utmost consequence.'*

Thus wrote

a woman, partly brave and partly good,
who fought with what she partly understood.
Few men about her would or could do more,
hence she was labelled harpy, shrew and whore.

8.

'You all die at fifteen,' said Diderot,
and turn part legend, part convention.
Still, eyes inaccurately dream
behind closed windows blankening with steam.
Deliciously, all that we might have been,
all that we were – fire, tears,
wit, taste, martyred ambition –
stirs like the memory of refused adultery
the drained and flagging bosom of our middle years.

9.

*Not that it is done well, but*
*that it is done at all?* Yes, think
of the odds! or shrug them off forever.
This luxury of the precocious child,
Time's precious chronic invalid, –
would we, darlings, resign it if we could?

Our blight has been our sinecure:
mere talent was enough for us –
glitter in fragments and rough drafts.

Sigh no more, ladies.
                              Time is male
and in his cups drinks to the fair.
Bemused by gallantry, we hear
our mediocrities over-praised,
indolence read as abnegation,
slattern thought styled intuition,
every lapse forgiven, our crime
only to cast too bold a shadow
or smash the mould straight off.

For that, solitary confinement,
tear gas, attrition shelling.
Few applicants for that honour.

10.

                              Well,
she's long about her coming, who must be
more merciless to herself than history.
Her mind full to the wind, I see her plunge
breasted and glancing through the currents,
taking the light upon her
at least as beautiful as any boy
or helicopter,
                    poised, still coming,
her fine blades making the air wince

but her cargo
no promise then:
delivered
palpable
ours.


*1958-1960*

# ANTINOÜS: THE DIARIES

Autumn torture. The old signs
smeared on the pavement, sopping leaves
rubbed into the landscape as unguent on a bruise,
brought indoors, even, as they bring flowers, enormous,
with the colours of the body's secret parts.
All this. And then, evenings, needing to be out,
walking fast, fighting the fire
that must die, light that sets my teeth on edge with joy,
till on the black embankment
I'm a cart stopped in the ruts of time.

Then at some house the rumour of truth and beauty
saturates a room like lilac-water
in the steam of a bath, fires snap, heads are high,
gold hair at napes of necks, gold in glasses,
gold in the throat, poetry of furs and manners.
Why do I shiver then? Haven't I seen,
over and over, before the end of an evening,
the three opened coffins carried in and left in a corner?
Haven't I watched as somebody cracked his shin
on one of them, winced and hopped and limped
laughing to lay his hand on a beautiful arm
striated with hairs of gold, like an almond-shell?

The old, needless story. For if I'm here
it is by choice and when at last
I smell my own rising nausea, feel the air
tighten around my stomach like a surgical bandage,

I can't pretend surprise.  What is it I so miscarry?
If what I spew on the tiles at last,
helpless, disgraced, alone,
is in part what I've swallowed from glasses, eyes,
motions of hands, opening and closing mouths,
isn't it also dead gobbets of myself,
abortive, murdered, or never willed?


*1959*

# THE ROOFWALKER

*for Denise Levertov*

Over the half-finished houses
night comes. The builders
stand on the roof. It is
quiet after the hammers,
the pulleys hang slack.
Giants, the roofwalkers,
on a listing deck, the wave
of darkness about to break
on their heads. The sky
is a torn sail where figures
pass magnified, shadows
on a burning deck.

I feel like them up there:
exposed, larger than life,
and due to break my neck.

Was it worth while to lay –
with infinite exertion –
a roof I can't live under?
 – All those blueprints,
closings of gaps,
measurings, calculations?
A life I didn't choose
chose me: even
my tools are the wrong ones

for what I have to do.
I'm naked, ignorant,
a naked man fleeing
across the roofs
who could with a shade of difference
be sitting in the lamplight
against the cream wallpaper
reading – not with indifference –
about a naked man
fleeing across the roofs.

*1961*

*from*

# *NECESSITIES OF LIFE*

(1966)

# IN THE WOODS

'Difficult ordinary happiness,'
no one nowadays believes in you.
I shift, full-length on the blanket,
to fix the sun precisely

behind the pine-tree's crest
so light spreads through the needles
alive as water just
where a snake has surfaced,

unreal as water in green crystal.
Bad news is always arriving.
'We're hiders, hiding from something bad,'
sings the little boy.

Writing these words in the woods,
I feel like a traitor to my friends,
even to my enemies.
The common lot's to die

a stranger's death and lie
rouged in the coffin, in a dress
chosen by the funeral director.
Perhaps that's why we never

see clocks on public buildings any more.
A fact no architect will mention.
We're hiders, hiding from something bad
most of the time.

Yet, and outrageously, something good
finds us, found me this morning
lying on a dusty blanket
among the burnt-out Indian pipes

and bursting-open lady's-slippers.
My soul, my helicopter, whirred
distantly, by habit, over
the old pond with the half-drowned boat

toward which it always veers
for consolation: ego's Arcady:
leaving the body stuck
like a leaf against a screen. –

Happiness! how many times
I've stranded on that word,
at the edge of that pond; seen
as if through tears, the dragon-fly –

only to find it all
going differently for once
this time: my soul wheeled back
and burst into my body.

Found! ready or not.
If I move now, the sun
naked between the trees
will melt me as I lie.

*1963*

# OPEN-AIR MUSEUM

Ailanthus, goldenrod, scrapiron, what makes you flower?
What burns in the dump today?

Thick flames in a grey field, tended
by two men: one derelict ghost,
one clearly apter at nursing destruction,
two priests in a grey field, tending the flames
of stripped-off rockwool, split
mattresses, a caved-in chickenhouse,
mad Lou's last stack of paintings, each a perfect black lozenge

seen from a train, stopped
as by design, to bring us
face to face with the flag of our true country:
violet-yellow, black-violet,
its heart sucked by slow fire
O my America
this then was your desire?

but you cannot burn fast enough:
in the photograph the white
skirts of the Harlem bride
are lashed by blown scraps, tabloid sheets,
and her beauty a scrap of flickering light
licked by a greater darkness

This then was your desire!
those trucked-off bad dreams
outside the city limits
crawl back in search of you, eyes
missing, skins missing, intenser in decay
the carriage that wheeled the defective baby
rolls up on three wheels
and the baby is still inside,
you cannot burn fast enough
Blue sparks of the chicory flower
flash from embers of the dump
inside the rose-rust carcass of a slaughtered Chevrolet
crouches the young ailanthus

and the two guardians go raking the sacred field, raking
slowly, to what endless end
Cry of truth among so many lies
at your heart burns on
a languid fire

*1964*

# NIGHT-PIECES: FOR A CHILD

*1. The Crib*

You sleeping I bend to cover.
Your eyelids work.  I see
your dream, cloudy as a negative,
swimming underneath.
You blurt a cry.  Your eyes
spring open, still filmed in dream.
Wider, they fix me –
 – death's head, sphinx, medusa?
You scream.
Tears lick my cheeks, my knees
droop at your fear.
Mother I no more am,
but woman, and nightmare.

*2. Her Waking*

Tonight I jerk astart in a dark
hourless as Hiroshima,
almost hearing you breathe
in a cot three doors away.

You still breathe, yes –
and my dream with its gift of knives,
its murderous hider and seeker,
ebbs away, recoils

back into the egg of dreams,
the vanishing point of mind.
All gone.

But you and I –
swaddled in a dumb dark
old as sickheartedness,
modern as pure annihilation –

we drift in ignorance.
If I could hear you now
mutter some gentle animal sound!
If milk flowed from my breast again . . . .


*1964*

# AUTUMN SEQUENCE

*1.*

An old shoe, an old pot, an old skin,
and dreams of the subtly tyrannical.
Thirst in the morning; waking into the blue

drought of another October
to read the familiar message nailed
to some burning bush or maple.

Breakfast under the pines, late yellow-
jackets fumbling for manna on the rim
of the stone crock of marmalade,

and shed pine-needles drifting
in the half-empty cup.
Generosity is drying out,

it's an act of will to remember
May's sticky-mouthed buds
on the provoked magnolias.

2.

Still, a sweetness hardly earned
by virtue or craft, belonging
by no desperate right to me

(as the marmalade to the wasp
who risked all in a last euphoria
of hunger)

washes the horizon. A quiet
after weeping, salt still on the tongue
is like this, when the autumn planet

looks me straight in the eye
and straight into the mind
plunges its impersonal spear:

*Fill and flow over, think*
*till you weep, then sleep*
*to drink again.*

3.

Your flag is dried-blood, turkey-comb
flayed stiff in the wind,
half-mast on the day of victory,

anarchist prince of evening marshes!
Your eye blurs in a wet smoke,
the stubble freezes under your heel,

the cornsilk *Mädchen* all hags now,
their gold teeth drawn,
the milkweeds gutted and rifled,

but not by you, foundering hero!
The future reconnoiters in dirty boots
along the cranberry-dark horizon.

Stars swim like grease-flecks
in that sky, night pulls a long knife.
Your empire drops to its knees in the dark.

4.

Skin of wet leaves on asphalt.
Charcoal slabs pitted with gold.
The reason for cities comes clear.

There must be a place, there has come a time –
where so many nerves are fusing –
for a purely moral loneliness.

Behind bloodsoaked lights of the avenues,
in the crystal grit of flying snow,
in this water-drop bulging at the taphead,

forced by dynamos three hundred miles
from the wild duck's landing and the otter's dive,
for three seconds of quivering identity.

There must be a place. But the eyeball stiffens
as night tightens and my hero passes out
with a film of stale gossip coating his tongue.

*1964*

## SPRING THUNDER

*1.*

Thunder is all it is, and yet
my street becomes a crack in the western hemisphere,
my house a fragile nest of grasses.

The radiotelescope flings its nets
at random; a child is crying,
not from hunger, not from pain,
more likely impotence.  The generals are sweltering

in the room with a thousand eyes.
Red-hot lights flash off and on
inside air-conditioned skulls.

Underfoot, a land-mass
puffed-up with bad faith and fatigue
goes lumbering onward,

old raft in the swollen waters,
unreformed Huck and Jim
watching the tangled yellow shores
rush by.

2.

Whatever you are that weeps
over the blistered riverbeds
and the cracked skin of cities,
you are not on our side,

eye never seeking our eyes,
shedding its griefs like stars
over our hectic indifference,
whispered monologue

subverting space with its tears,
mourning the mournable,
nailing the pale-grey woolly flower
back to its ledge.

3.

The power of the dinosaur
is ours, to die
inflicting death,
trampling the nested grasses:

power of dead grass
to catch fire
power of ash
to whirl off the burnt heap
in the wind's own time.

4.

A soldier is here, an ancient figure,
generalized as a basalt mask.

Breathes like a rabbit, an Eskimo,
strips to an older and simpler thing.

No criminal, no hero; merely a shadow
cast by the conflagration

that here burns down or there leaps higher
but always in the shape of fire,

always the method of fire, casting
automatically, these shadows.

5.

Over him, over you, a great roof is rising,
a great wall: no temporary shelter.
Did you tell yourself these beams would melt,

these fiery blocs dissolve?
Did you choose to build this thing?
Have you stepped back to see what it is?

It is immense; it has porches, catacombs.
It is provisioned like the Pyramids, for eternity.
Its buttresses beat back the air with iron tendons.

It is the first flying cathedral,
eating its parishes by the light of the moon.
It is the refinery of pure abstraction,

a total logic, rising
obscurely between one man
and the old, affective clouds.


*1965*

*from*

*LEAFLETS*

(1969)

# ORION

Far back when I went zig-zagging
through tamarack pastures
you were my genius, you
my cast-iron Viking, my helmed
lion-heart king in prison.
Years later now you're young

my fierce half-brother, staring
down from that simplified west
your breast open, your belt dragged down
by an oldfashioned thing, a sword
the last bravado you won't give over
though it weighs you down as you stride

and the stars in it are dim
and maybe have stopped burning.
But you burn, and I know it;
as I throw back my head to take you in
an old transfusion happens again:
divine astronomy is nothing to it.

Indoors I bruise and blunder,
break faith, leave ill enough
alone, a dead child born in the dark.
Night cracks up over the chimney,
pieces of time, frozen geodes
come showering down in the grate.

A man reaches behind my eyes
and finds them empty
a woman's head turns away
from my head in the mirror
children are dying my death
and eating crumbs of my life.

Pity is not your forte.
Calmly you ache up there
pinned aloft in your crow's nest,
my speechless pirate!
You take it all for granted
and when I look you back

it's with a starlike eye
shooting its cold and egotistical spear
where it can do least damage.
Breathe deep!  No hurt, no pardon
out here in the cold with you
you with your back to the wall.

*1965*

## JERUSALEM

In my dream, children
are stoning other children
with blackened carob-pods
I dream my son is riding
on an old grey mare
to a half-dead war
on a dead-grey road
through the cactus and thistles
and dried brook-beds.

In my dream, children
are swaddled in smoke
and their uncut hair smoulders
even here, here
where trees have no shade
and rocks have no shadow
trees have no memories
only the stones and
the hairs of the head.

I dream his hair is growing
and has never been shorn
from slender temples hanging
like curls of barbed wire
and his first beard is growing
smouldering like fire
his beard is smoke and fire
and I dream him riding
patiently to the war.

47

What I dream of the city
is how hard it is to leave
and how useless to walk
outside the blasted walls
picking up the shells
from a half-dead war
and I wake up in tears
and hear the sirens screaming
and the carob-tree is bare.


*Balfour Street*
*July 1966*

## THE BREAK

All month eating the heart out,
smothering in a fierce insomnia . . .
First the long, spongy summer, drying
out by fits and starts, till a morning
torn off another calendar
when the wind stiffens, chairs
and tables rouse themselves
in a new, unplanned light
and a word flies like a dry leaf down the hall
at the bang of a door.

Then break, October, speak,
non-existent and damning clarity.
Stare me down, thrust
your tongue against mine, break
day, let me stand up
like a table or a chair
in a cold room with the sun beating in
full on the dusty panes.


*1967*

## THE KEY

Through a drain grating, something
     glitters and falters,
          glitters again.  A scrap of foil,

a coin, a signal, a message
     from the indistinct
          piercing my indistinctness?

How long I have gone round
     and round, spiritless with foreknown defeat,
          in search of that glitter?

Hours, years maybe.  The cry of metal
     on asphalt, on iron, the sudden
          *ching* of a precious loss,

the clear statement
     of something missing.  Over and over
          it stops me in my tracks

like a falling star, only
     this is not the universe's loss
          it is mine.  If I were only colder,

nearer death, nearer birth, I might let go
     whatever's so bent on staying lost.
          Why not leave the house

locked, to collapse inward among its weeds,
      the letters to darken and flake
            in the drawer, the car

to grow skeletal, aflame with rust
      in the moonlit lot, and walk
            ever after?

O God I am not spiritless,
      but a spirit can be stunned,
            a battery felt going dead

before the light flickers,
      and I've covered this ground too often
            with this yellow disc

within whose beam all's commonplace
      and whose limits are described
            by the whole night.


*1967*

# TO FRANTZ FANON

*Born Martinique, 1925; dead Washington D.C., 1961*


I don't see your head
sunk, listening     to the throats
of the torturers and the tortured

I don't see your eyes
deep in the blackness     of your skull
they look off from me     into the eyes

of rats and haunted policemen.
What I see best is the length
of your fingers
pressing the pencil
into the barred page

of the French child's copybook
with its Cartesian squares     its grilled
trap of holy geometry
where your night-sweats streamed out
in language

and your death
a black streak on a white bed
in L'Enfant's city where
the fever-bush sweats off

its thick
petals    year after year
on the mass grave
of revolt

*1968*

*from*

## THE WILL TO CHANGE

(1971)

# PLANETARIUM

*Thinking of Caroline Herschel (1750-1848) astronomer,*
*sister of William; and others.*


A woman in the shape of a monster
a monster in the shape of a woman
the skies are full of them

a woman     'in the snow
among the Clocks and instruments
or measuring the ground with poles'

in her 98 years to discover
8 comets

she whom the moon ruled
like us
levitating into the night sky
riding the polished lenses

Galaxies of women, there
doing penance for impetuousness
ribs chilled
in those spaces     of the mind

An eye,
        'virile, precise and absolutely certain'
        from the mad webs of Uranusborg
                            encountering the NOVA

every impulse of light exploding
from the core
as life flies out of us

      Tycho whispering at last
      'Let me not seem to have lived in vain'

What we see, we see
and seeing is changing

the light that shrivels a mountain
and leaves a man alive

Heartbeat of the pulsar
heart sweating through my body

The radio impulse
pouring in from Taurus

      I am bombarded yet    I stand

I have been standing all my life in the
direct path of a battery of signals
the most accurately transmitted most
untranslatable language in the universe
I am a galactic cloud so deep   so invo-
luted that a light wave could take 15
years to travel through me   And has
taken   I am an instrument in the shape
of a woman trying to translate pulsations
into images   for the relief of the body
and the reconstruction of the mind.

*1968*

# I DREAM I'M THE DEATH OF ORPHEUS

I am walking rapidly through striations of light and dark
　　　　thrown under an arcade.

I am a woman in the prime of life, with certain powers
and those powers severely limited
by authorities whose faces I rarely see.
I am a woman in the prime of life
driving her dead poet in a black Rolls-Royce
through a landscape of twilight and thorns.
A woman with a certain mission
which if obeyed to the letter will leave her intact.
A woman with the nerves of a panther
a woman with contacts among Hell's Angels
a woman feeling the fullness of her powers
at the precise moment when she must not use them
a woman sworn to lucidity
who sees through the mayhem, the smoky fires
of these underground streets
her dead poet learning to walk backward against the wind
on the wrong side of the mirror

*1968*

## *from* THE BLUE GHAZALS

*9/28/68: I*

A man, a woman, a city.
The city as object of love.

Anger and filth in the basement.
The furnace stoked and blazing.

A sexual heat on the pavements.
Trees erected like statues.

Eyes at the ends of avenues.
Yellow for hesitation.

I'm tired of walking your streets
he says, unable to leave her.

Air of dust and rising sparks,
the city burning her letters.

*9/28/68: II*

*for Wallace Stevens*


Ideas of order . . . Sinner of the Florida keys,
you were our poet of revolution all along.

A man isn't what he seems but what he desires:
gaieties of anarchy drumming at the base of the skull.

Would this have left you cold, our scene, its wild parades,
the costumes, banners, incense, flowers, the immense marches?

Disorder is natural, these leaves absently blowing
in the drinking-fountain, filling the statue's crevice.

The use of force in public architecture:
nothing, not even the honeycomb, manifests such control.


*12/13/68*

They say, if you can tell, clasped tight under the blanket,
the edge of dark from the edge of dawn, your love is a lie.

If I thought of my words as changing minds,
hadn't my mind also to suffer changes?

They measure fever, swab the blisters of the throat,
but the cells of thought go rioting on ignored.

It's the inner ghost that suffers, little spirit
looking out wildly from the clouded pupils.

When will we lie clearheaded in our flesh again
with the cold edge of the night driving us close together?


*5/4/69*

Pain made her conservative.
Where the matches touched her flesh, she wears a scar.

The police arrive at dawn
like death and childbirth.

City of accidents, your true map
is the tangling of all our lifelines.

*The moment when a feeling enters the body*
is political.  This touch is political.

Sometimes I dream we are floating on water
hand-in-hand; and sinking without terror.

# OUR WHOLE LIFE

Our whole life a translation
the permissible fibs

and now a knot of lies
eating at itself to get undone

Words bitten thru words

meanings burnt-off like paint
under the blowtorch

All those dead letters
rendered into the oppressor's language

Trying to tell the doctor where it hurts
like the Algerian
who has walked from his village, burning

his whole body a cloud of pain
and there are no words for this

except himself

*1969*

# THE STELAE

*for Arnold Rich*


Last night I met you in my sister's house
risen from the dead
showing me your collection

You are almost at the point of giving things away

It's the stelae on the walls I want
that I never saw before

You offer other objects
I have seen time and time again

I think you think you are giving me
something precious

The stelae are so unlike you
swart, indifferent, incised with signs
you have never deciphered

I never knew you had them
I wonder if you are giving them away


*1969*

*from*

# DIVING INTO THE WRECK

*(1973)*

# DIVING INTO THE WRECK

First having read the book of myths,
and loaded the camera,
and checked the edge of the knife-blade,
I put on
the body-armour of black rubber
the absurd flippers
the grave and awkward mask.
I am having to do this
not like Cousteau with his
assiduous team
aboard the sun-flooded schooner
but here alone.

There is a ladder.
The ladder is always there
hanging innocently
close to the side of the schooner.
We know what it is for,
we who have used it.
Otherwise
it's a piece of maritime floss
some sundry equipment.

I go down.
Rung after rung and still
the oxygen immerses me
the blue light
the clear atoms

of our human air.
I go down.
My flippers cripple me,
I crawl like an insect down the ladder
and there is no one
to tell me when the ocean
will begin.

First the air is blue and then
it is bluer and then green and then
black I am blacking out and yet
my mask is powerful
it pumps my blood with power
the sea is another story
the sea is not a question of power
I have to learn alone
to turn my body without force
in the deep element.

And now: it is easy to forget
what I came for
among so many who have always
lived here
swaying their crenellated fans
between the reefs
and besides
you breathe differently down here.

I came to explore the wreck.
The words are purposes.
The words are maps.

I came to see the damage that was done
and the treasures that prevail.
I stroke the beam of my lamp
slowly along the flank
of something more permanent
than fish or weed

the thing I came for:
the wreck and not the story of the wreck
the thing itself and not the myth
the drowned face always staring
toward the sun
the evidence of damage
worn by salt and sway into this threadbare beauty
the ribs of the disaster
curving their assertion
among the tentative haunters.

This is the place.
And I am here, the mermaid whose dark hair
streams black, the merman in his armoured body
We circle silently
about the wreck
we dive into the hold.
I am she: I am he

whose drowned face sleeps with open eyes
whose breasts still bear the stress
whose silver, copper, vermeil cargo lies
obscurely inside barrels
half-wedged and left to rot

we are the half-destroyed instruments
that once held to a course
the water-eaten log
the fouled compass

We are, I am, you are
by cowardice or courage
the one who find our way
back to this scene
carrying a knife, a camera
a book of myths
in which
our names do not appear.


1972

# SONG

You're wondering if I'm lonely:
OK then, yes, I'm lonely
as a plane rides lonely and level
on its radio beam, aiming
across the Rockies
for the blue-strung aisles
of an airfield on the ocean

You want to ask, am I lonely?
Well, of course, lonely
as a woman driving across country
day after day, leaving behind
mile after mile
little towns she might have stopped
and lived and died in, lonely

If I'm lonely
it must be the loneliness
of waking first, of breathing
dawn's first cold breath on the city
of being the one awake
in a house wrapped in sleep

If I'm lonely
it's with the rowboat ice-fast on the shore
in the last red light of the year
that knows what it is, that knows it's neither
ice nor mud nor winter light
but wood, with a gift for burning

*1971*

# MERCED

Fantasies of old age:
they have rounded us up
in a rest-camp for the outworn.
Somewhere in some dustbowl
a barbed-wire cantonment
of low-cost dustcoloured prefab
buildings, smelling of shame
and hopeless incontinence
identical clothes of disposable
paper, identical rations
of chemically flavoured food
Death in order, by gas,
hypodermics daily
to neutralize despair
So I imagine my world
in my seventieth year alive
and outside the barbed wire
a purposeless exchange
of consciousness for the absence
of pain. We will call this life.

Yet only last summer I
burned my feet in the sand
of that valley traced by the thread
of the cold quick river Merced
watered by plummets of white
When I swam, my body ached
from the righteous cold

when I lay back floating the jays
flittered from pine to pine
and the shade moved hour by hour
across El Capitan
Our wine cooled in the water
and I watched my sons, half-men
half-children, testing their part
in a world almost archaic
so precious by this time
that merely to step in pure water
or stare into clean air
is to feel a spasm of pain.

For weeks now a rage
has possessed my body, driving
now out upon men and women
now inward upon myself
Walking Amsterdam Avenue
I find myself in tears
without knowing which thought
forced water to my eyes
To speak to another human
becomes a risk
I think of Norman Morrison
the Buddhists of Saigon
the black teacher last week
who put himself to death
to waken guilt in hearts
too numb to get the message
in a world masculinity made

unfit for women or men
Taking off in a plane
I look down at the city
which meant life to me, not death
and think that somewhere there
a cold centre, composed
of pieces of human beings
metabolized, restructured
by a process they do not feel
is spreading in our midst
and taking over our minds
a thing that feels neither guilt
nor rage: that is unable
to hate, therefore to love.


*1972*

# BURNING ONESELF IN

In a bookstore on the East Side
I read a veteran's testimony:

the running down, for no reason,
of an old woman in South Vietnam
by a U.S. Army truck

The heat-wave is over
Lifeless, sunny, the East Side
rests under its awnings

Another summer
The flames go on feeding

and a dull heat permeates the ground
of the mind, the burn has settled in
as if it had no more question

of its right to go on devouring
the rest of a lifetime,
the rest of history

Pieces of information, like this one
blow onto the heap

they keep it fed, whether we will it or not,
another summer, and another
of suffering quietly

in bookstores, in the parks
however we may scream we are
suffering quietly

*1972*

*from*

*THE FACT OF A DOORFRAME*

*Poems: Selected & New 1950-1984*

(1984)

# AT THE JEWISH NEW YEAR

For more than five thousand years
This calm September day
With yellow in the leaf
Has lain in the kernel of Time
While the world outside the walls
Has had its turbulent say
And history like a long
Snake has crawled on its way
And is crawling onward still.
And we have little to tell
On this or any feast
Except of the terrible past.
Five thousand years are cast
Down before the wondering child
Who must expiate them all.

Some of us have replied
In the bitterness of youth
Or the qualms of middle-age:
'If Time is unsatisfied,
And all our fathers have suffered
Can never be enough,
Why, then, we choose to forget.
Let our forgetting begin
With those age-old arguments
In which their minds were wound
Like musty phylacteries;
And we choose to forget as well

Those cherished histories
That made our old men fond,
And already are strange to us.

'Or let us, being today
Too rational to cry out,
Or trample underfoot
What after all preserves
A certain savour yet –
Though torn up by the roots –
Let us make our compromise
With the terror and the guilt
And view as curious relics
Once found in daily use
The mythology, the names
That, however Time has corrupted
Their ancient purity
Still burn like yellow flames,
But their fire is not for us.'

And yet, however we choose
To deny or to remember,
Though on the calendars
We wake and suffer by,
This day is merely one
Of thirty in September –
In the kernel of the mind
The new year must renew
This day, as for our kind
Over five thousand years,
The task of being ourselves.

Whatever we strain to forget,
Our memory must be long.

May the taste of honey linger
Under the bitterest tongue.


*1955*

# DIEN BIEN PHU

A nurse on the battlefield
wounded herself, but working

    dreams
        that each man she touches
        is a human grenade

            an anti-personnel weapon
            that can explode in her arms

    How long
        can she go on like this
        putting mercy
        ahead of survival

She is walking
in a white dress stained
with earth and blood

        down a road lined
        with fields long
        given up        blasted

        cemeteries of one name
        or two

    A hand
    juts out like barbed wire
    it is terribly alone

if she takes it

        will it slash her wrists again

if she passes it by

        will she turn into a case
        of shell-shock, eyes
        glazed forever on the

                blank chart of
                amnesia

*1973*

*from*

# THE DREAM OF A

# COMMON LANGUAGE

*(1978)*

# POWER

Living      in the earth-deposits     of our history

Today a backhoe divulged    out of a crumbling flank of earth
one bottle     amber     perfect     a hundred-year-old
cure for fever    or melancholy     a tonic
for living on this earth     in the winters of this climate

Today I was reading about Marie Curie:
she must have known she suffered     from radiation sickness
her body bombarded for years     by the element
she had purified
It seems she denied to the end
the source of the cataracts on her eyes
the cracked and suppurating skin     of her finger-ends
till she could no longer hold     a test-tube or a pencil

She died     a famous woman     denying
her wounds
denying
her wounds     came     from the same source as her power

*1974*

# *from* TWENTY-ONE LOVE POEMS

*I*

Wherever in this city, screens flicker
with pornography, with science-fiction vampires,
victimized hirelings bending to the lash,
we also have to walk . . . if simply as we walk
through the rainsoaked garbage, the tabloid cruelties
of our own neighbourhoods.
We need to grasp our lives inseparable
from those rancid dreams, that blurt of metal, those disgraces,
and the red begonia perilously flashing
from a tenement sill six stories high,
or the long-legged young girls playing ball
in the junior highschool playground.
No one has imagined us.  We want to live like trees,
sycamores blazing through the sulfuric air,
dappled with scars, still exuberantly budding,
our animal passion rooted in the city.


*VII*

What kind of beast would turn its life into words?
What atonement is this all about?
 – and yet, writing words like these, I'm also living.
Is all this close to the wolverines' howled signals,
that modulated cantata of the wild?
or, when away from you I try to create you in words,

am I simply using you, like a river or a war?
And how have I used rivers, how have I used wars
to escape writing of the worst thing of all –
not the crimes of others, not even our own death,
but the failure to want our freedom passionately enough
so that blighted elms, sick rivers, massacres would seem
mere emblems of that desecration of ourselves?


*XII*


Sleeping, turning in turn like planets
rotating in their midnight meadow:
a touch is enough to let us know
we're not alone in the universe, even in sleep:
the dream-ghosts of two worlds
walking their ghost-towns, almost address each other.
I've wakened to your muttered words
spoken light- or dark-years away
as if my own voice had spoken.
But we have different voices, even in sleep,
and our bodies, so alike, are yet so different
and the past echoing through our bloodstreams
is freighted with different language, different meanings –
though in any chronicle of the world we share
it could be written with new meaning
we were two lovers of one gender,
we were two women of one generation.

## XX

That conversation we were always on the edge
of having, runs on in my head,
at night the Hudson trembles in New Jersey light
polluted water yet reflecting even
sometimes the moon
and I discern a woman
I loved, drowning in secrets, fear wound round her throat
and choking her like hair. And this is she
with whom I tried to speak, whose hurt, expressive head
turning aside from pain, is dragged down deeper
where it cannot hear me,
and soon I shall know I was talking to my own soul.


## XXI

The dark lintels, the blue and foreign stones
of the great round rippled by stone implements
the midsummer night light rising from beneath
the horizon – when I said 'a cleft of light'
I meant this. And this is not Stonehenge
simply nor any place but the mind
casting back to where her solitude,
shared, could be chosen without loneliness,
not easily nor without pains to stake out
the circle, the heavy shadows, the great light.
I choose to be a figure in that light,
half-blotted by darkness, something moving

across that space, the colour of stone
greeting the moon, yet more than stone:
a woman.  I choose to walk here.  And to draw this circle.


*1974-1976*

# TOWARD THE SOLSTICE

The thirtieth of November.
Snow is starting to fall.
A peculiar silence is spreading
over the fields, the maple grove.
It is the thirtieth of May,
rain pours on ancient bushes, runs
down the youngest blade of grass.
I am trying to hold in one steady glance
all the parts of my life.
A spring torrent races
on this old slanting roof,
the slanted field below
thickens with winter's first whiteness.
Thistles dried to sticks in last year's wind
stand nakedly in the green,
stand sullenly in the slowly whitening,
field.

      My brain glows
more violently, more avidly
the quieter, the thicker
the quilt of crystals settles,
the louder, more relentlessly
the torrent beats itself out
on the old boards and shingles.
It is the thirtieth of May,
the thirtieth of November,
a beginning or an end,

we are moving into the solstice
and there is so much here
I still do not understand.

If I could make sense of how
my life is still tangled
with dead weeds, thistles,
enormous burdocks, burdens
slowly shifting under
this first fall of snow,
beaten by this early, racking rain
calling all new life to declare itself strong
or die,
       if I could know
in what language to address
the spirits that claim a place
beneath these low and simple ceilings,
tenants that neither speak nor stir
yet dwell in mute insistence
till I can feel utterly ghosted in this house.

If history is a spider-thread
spun over and over though brushed away
it seems I might some twilight
or dawn in the hushed country light
discern its greyness stretching
from moulding or doorframe, out
into the empty dooryard
and following it climb
the path into the pinewoods,
tracing from tree to tree

in the failing light, in the slowly
lucidifying day
its constant, purposive trail,
till I reach whatever cellar hole
filling with snowflakes or lichen,
whatever fallen shack
or unremembered clearing
I am meant to have found
and there, under the first or last
star, trusting to instinct
the words would come to mind
I have failed or forgotten to say
year after year, winter
after summer, the right rune
to ease the hold of the past
upon the rest of my life
and ease my hold on the past.

If some rite of separation
is still unaccomplished
between myself and the long-gone
tenants of this house,
between myself and my childhood,
and the childhood of my children,
it is I who have neglected
to perform the needed acts,
set water in corners, light and eucalyptus
in front of mirrors,
or merely pause and listen
to my own pulse vibrating

lightly as falling snow,
relentlessly as the rainstorm,
and hear what it has been saying.
It seems I am still waiting
for them to make some clear demand
some articulate sound or gesture,
for release to come from anywhere
but from inside myself.

A decade of cutting away
dead flesh, cauterizing
old scars ripped open over and over
and still it is not enough.
A decade of performing
the loving humdrum acts
of attention to this house
transplanting lilac suckers,
washing panes, scrubbing
wood-smoke from splitting paint,
sweeping stairs, brushing the thread
of the spider aside,
and so much yet undone,
a woman's work, the solstice nearing,
and my hand still suspended
as if above a letter
I long and dread to close.

*1977*

*from*

*A WILD PATIENCE HAS*

*TAKEN ME THIS FAR*

*(1981)*

# INTEGRITY

*the quality or state of being complete; unbroken condition; entirety*
    *— Webster*


A wild patience has taken me this far

as if I had to bring to shore
a boat with a spasmodic outboard motor
old sweaters, nets, spray-mottled books
tossed in the prow
some kind of sun burning my shoulder-blades.
Splashing the oarlocks.  Burning through.
Your fore-arms can get scalded, licked with pain
in a sun blotted like unspoken anger
behind a casual mist.

The length of daylight
this far north, in this
forty-ninth year of my life
is critical.

The light is critical: of me, of this
long-dreamed, involuntary landing
on the arm of an inland sea.
The glitter of the shoal
depleting into shadow
I recognise: the stand of pines
violet-black really, green in the old postcard
but really I have nothing but myself

to go by; nothing
stands in the realm of pure necessity
except what my hands can hold.

*Nothing but myself? ... My selves.*
After so long, this answer.
As if I had always known
I steer the boat in, simply.
The motor dying on the pebbles
cicadas taking up the hum
dropped in the silence.

Anger and tenderness: my selves.
And now I can believe they breathe in me
as angels, not polarities.
Anger and tenderness: the spider's genius
to spin and weave in the same action
from her own body, anywhere –
even from a broken web.

The cabin in the stand of pines
is still for sale. I know this. Know the print
of the last foot, the hand that slammed and locked that door,
then stopped to wreathe the rain-smashed clematis
back on the trellis
for no one's sake except its own.
I know the chart nailed to the wallboards
the icy kettle squatting on the burner.
The hands that hammered in those nails
emptied that kettle one last time
are these two hands

and they have caught the baby leaping
from between trembling legs
and they have worked the vacuum aspirator
and stroked the sweated temples
and steered the boat here through this hot
mistblotted sunlight, critical light
imperceptibly scalding
the skin these hands will also salve.


*1978*

## FOR MEMORY

Old words:   *trust   fidelity*
Nothing new yet to take their place.

I rake leaves, clear the lawn, October grass
painfully green beneath the gold
and in this silent labour thoughts of you
start up
I hear your voice:   *disloyalty   betrayal*
stinging the wires

I stuff the old leaves into sacks
and still they fall and still
I see my work undone

One shivering rainswept afternoon
and the whole job to be done over

I can't know what you know
unless you tell me
there are gashes in our understandings
of this world
We came together in a common
fury of direction
barely mentioning difference
(what drew our finest hairs
to fire
the deep, difficult troughs
unvoiced)

I fell through a basement railing
the first day of school and cut my forehead open –
did I ever tell you?  More than forty years
and I still remember smelling my own blood
like the smell of a new schoolbook

And did you ever tell me
how your mother called you in from play
and from whom?  To what?  These atoms filmed by
          ordinary dust
that common life we each and all bent out of orbit from
to which we must return simply to say
*this is where I came from*
*this is what I knew*

The past is not a husk     yet change goes on

Freedom.  It isn't once, to walk out
under the Milky Way, feeling the rivers
of light, the fields of dark –
freedom is daily, prose-bound, routine
remembering.  Putting together, inch by inch
the starry worlds.  From all the lost collections.


*1979*

# FOR ETHEL ROSENBERG

*convicted, with her husband,*
*of 'conspiracy to commit*
*espionage'; killed in the*
*electric chair June 19, 1953*


*1.*


Europe 1953:
throughout my random sleepwalk
the words

scratched on walls, on pavements
painted over railway arches
*Liberez les Rosenberg!*

Escaping from home I found
home everywhere:
the Jewish question, Communism

marriage itself
a question of loyalty
or punishment

my Jewish father writing me
letters of seventeen pages
finely inscribed harangues

questions of loyalty
and punishment
One week before my wedding

that couple gets the chair
the volts grapple her, don't
kill her fast enough

*Liberez les Rosenberg!*
I hadn't realized
our family arguments were so important

my narrow understanding
of crime     of punishment
no language for this torment

mystery of that marriage
always both faces
on every front page in the world

Something so shocking     so
unfathomable
it must be pushed aside


2.


She sank however into my soul     A weight of sadness
I hardly can register how deep
her memory has sunk     that wife and mother

like so many
who seemed to get nothing out of any of it
except her children

that daughter     of a family
like so many
needing its female monster

she, actually wishing to be     *an artist*
wanting out of poverty
possibly also really wanting

                              revolution

that woman     strapped in the chair
*no fear and no regrets*
charged by posterity

not with selling secrets to the Communists
but with wanting     *to distinguish*
*herself*     being a bad daughter     a bad mother

And I     walking to my wedding
by the same token a bad daughter     a bad sister
my forces focussed

on that hardly revolutionary effort
Her life and death     the possible
ranges of disloyalty

so painful     so unfathomable
they must be pushed aside
ignored for years

3.

Her mother testifies against her
Her brother testifies against her
After her death

she becomes a natural prey for pornographers
her death itself a scene
her body *sizzling    half-strapped    whipped like a sail*

She becomes the extremest victim
described nonetheless as *rigid of will*
what are her politics by then    no one knows

Her figure sinks into my soul
a drowned statue
sealed in lead

For years it has lain there    unabsorbed
first as part of that dead couple
on the front pages of the world    the week

I gave myself in marriage
then slowly severing    drifting apart
a separate death    a life unto itself

no longer *the Rosenbergs*
no longer the chosen scapegoat
the family monster

till I hear how she sang
a prostitute to sleep
in the Women's House of Detention

Ethel Greenglass Rosenberg    would you
have marched to take back the night
collected signatures

for battered women who kill
What would you have to tell us
would you have burst the net


4.


Why do I even want to call her up
to console my pain    (she feels no pain at all)
why do I wish to put such questions

to ease myself    (she feels no pain at all
she    finally burned to death    like so many)
why all this exercise of hindsight?

since    if I imagine her at all
I have to imagine first
the pain inflicted on her    by women

*her mother testifies against her*
*her sister-in-law testifies against her*
and how she sees it

not the impersonal forces
not the historical reasons
why they might have hated her strength

If I have held her at arm's length till now
if I have still believed it was
my loyalty, my punishment at stake

if I dare imagine her surviving
I must be fair to what she must have lived through
I must allow her to be at last

political in her ways     not in mine
her urgencies perhaps     impervious to mine
defining revolution as she defines it

or, bored to the marrow of her bones
with 'politics'
bored with the vast boredom of long pain

small; tiny in fact; in her late sixties
liking her room     her private life
living alone perhaps

no one you could interview
maybe filling a notebook herself
with secrets she has never sold


*1980*

# FRAME

Winter twilight.  She comes out of the lab-
oratory, last class of the day
a pile of notebooks slung in her knapsack, coat
zipped high against the already swirling
evening sleet.  The wind is wicked and the
busses slower than usual.  On her mind
is organic chemistry and the issue
of next month's rent and will it be possible to
bypass the professor with the coldest eyes
to get a reference for graduate school,
and whether any of them, even those who smile
can see, looking at her, a biochemist
or a marine biologist, which of the faces
can she trust to see her at all, either today
or in any future.  The busses are worm-slow in the
quickly gathering dark.  *I don't know her. I am*
*standing though somewhere just outside the frame*
*of all this, trying to see.*  At her back
the newly finished building suddenly looks
like shelter, it has glass doors, lighted halls
presumably heat.  The wind is wicked.  She throws a
glance down the street, sees no bus coming and runs
up the newly constructed steps into the newly
constructed hallway.  *I am standing all this time*
*just beyond the frame, trying to see.*  She runs
her hand through the crystals of sleet about to melt
on her hair.  She shifts the weight of the books
on her back.  It isn't warm here exactly but it's

out of that wind.  Through the glass
door panels she can watch for the bus through the thickening
weather.  Watching so, she is not
watching for the white man who watches the building
who has been watching her.  This is Boston 1979.
*I am standing somewhere at the edge of the frame*
*watching the man, we are both white, who watches the building*
*telling her to move on,  get out of the hallway.*
*I can hear nothing because I am not supposed to be*
*present but I can see her gesturing*
*out toward the street at the wind-raked curb*
*I see her drawing her small body up*
*against the implied charges.*  The man
goes away.  Her body is different now.
It is holding together with more than a hint of fury
and more than a hint of fear.  She is smaller, thinner
more fragile-looking than I am.  *But I am not supposed to be*
*there.  I am just outside the frame*
*of this action when the anonymous white man*
*returns with a white police officer.*  Then she starts
to leave into the windraked night but already
the policeman is going to work, the handcuffs are on her
wrists he is throwing her down his knee has gone into
her breast he is dragging her down the stairs *I am unable*
*to hear a sound of all this all that I know is what*
*I can see from this position there is no soundtrack*
*to go with this and I understand at once*
*it is meant to be in silence that this happens*
in silence that he pushes her into the car
banging her head in silence that she cries out
in silence that she tries to explain she was only

waiting for a bus
in silence that he twists the flesh of her thigh
with his nails in silence that her tears begin to flow
that she pleads with the other policeman as if
he could be trusted to see her at all
in silence that in the precinct she refuses to give her name
in silence that they throw her into the cell
in silence that she stares him
straight in the face in silence that he sprays her
in her eyes with Mace in silence that she sinks her teeth
into his hand in silence that she is charged
with trespass assault and battery in
silence that at the sleet-swept corner her bus
passes without stopping and goes on
in silence. *What I am telling you*
*is told by a white woman who they will say*
*was never there. I say I am there.*


*1980*

## *from* TURNING THE WHEEL

### 5. *Particularity*

In search of the desert witch, the shamaness
forget the archetypes, forget the dark
and lithic profile, do not scan the clouds
massed on the horizon, violet and green,
for her icon, do not pursue
the ready-made abstraction, do not peer for symbols.
So long as you want her faceless, without smell
or voice, so long as she does not squat
to urinate, or scratch herself, so long
as she does not snore beneath her blanket
or grimace as she grasps the stone-cold
grinding stone at dawn
so long as she does not have her own peculiar
face, slightly wall-eyed or with a streak
of topaz lightning in the blackness
of one eye, so long as she does not limp
so long as you try to simplify her meaning
so long as she merely symbolizes power
she is kept helpless and conventional
her true power routed backward
into the past, we cannot touch or name her
and, barred from participation by those who need her
she stifles in unspeakable loneliness.

## 8. *Turning the Wheel*

The road to the great canyon always feels
like that road and no other
the highway to a fissure    to the female core
of a continent
Below Flagstaff even    the rock erosions wear
a famous handwriting
the river's still prevailing signature

Seeing those rocks    that road    in dreams    I know
it is happening again    as twice while waking
I am travelling to the edge    to meet the face
of annihilating and impersonal time
stained in the colours of a woman's genitals
outlasting every transient violation
a face that is strangely intimate to me

Today I turned the wheel    refused that journey
I was feeling too alone on the open plateau
of piñon juniper    world beyond time
of rockflank spread around me    too alone
and too filled with you    with whom I talked for hours
driving up from the desert    though you were far away
as I talk to you all day    whatever day

*1981*

*from*

*YOUR NATIVE LAND,*

*YOUR LIFE*

*(1986)*

# NORTH AMERICAN TIME

*I*

When my dreams showed signs
of becoming
politically correct
no unruly images
escaping beyond borders
when walking in the street I found my
themes cut out for me
knew what I would not report
for fear of enemies' usage
then I began to wonder

*II*

Everything we write
will be used against us
or against those we love.
These are the terms,
take them or leave them.
Poetry never stood a chance
of standing outside history.
One line typed twenty years ago
can be blazed on a wall in spraypaint
to glorify art as detachment
or torture of those we
did not love but also
did not want to kill

We move    but our words stand
become responsible
for more than we intended

and this is verbal privilege

*III*

Try sitting at a typewriter
one calm summer evening
at a table by a window
in the country, try pretending
your time does not exist
that you are simply you
that the imagination simply strays
like a great moth, unintentional
try telling yourself
you are not accountable
to the life of your tribe
the breath of your planet

*IV*

It doesn't matter what you think.
Words are found responsible
all you can do is choose them
or choose
to remain silent.    Or, you never had a choice,
which is why the words that do stand
are responsible

and this is verbal privilege

*V*

Suppose you want to write
of a woman braiding
another woman's hair –
straight down, or with beads and shells
in three-strand plaits or corn-rows –
you had better know the thickness
the length     the pattern
why she decides to braid her hair
how it is done to her
what country it happens in
what else happens in that country

You have to know these things

*VI*

Poet, sister:     words –
whether we like it or not –
stand in a time of their own.
No use protesting     *I wrote that*
*before Kollontai was exiled*
*Rosa Luxemburg, Malcolm,*
*Anna Mae Aquash, murdered,*
*before Treblinka, Birkenau,*
*Hiroshima, before Sharpeville,*
*Biafra, Bangladesh, Boston,*
*Atlanta, Soweto, Beirut, Assam*
– those faces, names of places
sheared from the almanac
of North American time

*VII*

I am thinking this in a country
where words are stolen out of mouths
as bread is stolen out of mouths
where poets don't go to jail
for being poets, but for being
dark-skinned, female, poor.
I am writing this in a time
when anything we write
can be used against those we love
where the context is never given
though we try to explain, over and over
For the sake of poetry at least
I need to know these things

*VIII*

Sometimes, gliding at night
in a plane over New York City
I have felt like some messenger
called to enter, called to engage
this field of light and darkness.
A grandiose idea, born of flying.
But underneath the grandiose idea
is the thought that what I must engage
after the plane has raged onto the tarmac
after climbing my old stairs, sitting down
at my old window
is meant to break my heart and reduce me to silence.

*IX*

In North America time stumbles on
without moving, only releasing
a certain North American pain.
Julia de Burgos wrote:
*That my grandfather was a slave*
*is my grief; had he been a master*
*that would have been my shame.*
A poet's words, hung over a door
in North America, in the year
nineteen-eighty-three.
The almost-full moon rises
timelessly speaking of change
out of the Bronx, the Harlem River
the drowned towns of the Quabbin
the pilfered burial mounds
the toxic swamps, the testing-grounds

and I start to speak again.


*1983*

# BLUE ROCK

*for Myriam Díaz-Diocaretz*

Your chunk of lapis-lazuli shoots its stain
blue into the wineglass on the table

the full moon moving up the sky is plain
as the dead rose and the live buds on one stem

No, this isn't Persian poetry I'm quoting:
all this is here in North America

where I sit trying to kindle fire
from what's already on fire:

the light of a blue rock from Chile swimming
in the apricot liquid called 'eye of the swan'.


This is a chunk of your world, a piece of its heart:
split from the rest, does it suffer?

You needn't tell me.   Sometimes I hear it singing
by the waters of Babylon, in a strange land

sometimes it just lies heavy in my hand
with the heaviness of silent seismic knowledge

a blue rock in a foreign land, an exile
excised but never separated

from the gashed heart, its mountains,
winter rains, language, native sorrow.


At the end of the twentieth century
cardiac graphs of torture reply to poetry

line by line:     in North America
the strokes of the stylus continue

the figures of terror are reinvented
all night, after I turn the lamp off, blotting

wineglass, rock and roses, leaving pages
like this scrawled with mistakes and love,

falling asleep; but the stylus does not sleep,
cruelly the drum revolves, cruelty writes its name.


Once when I wrote poems they did not change
left overnight on the page

they stayed as they were and daylight broke
on the lines, as on the clotheslines in the yard

heavy with clothes forgotten or left out
for a better sun next day

But now I know what happens while I sleep
and when I wake the poem has changed:

the facts have dilated it, or cancelled it;
and in every morning's light, your rock is there.


*1985*

# VIRGINIA 1906

A white woman dreaming of innocence,
of a country childhood, apple-blossom driftings,
is held in a DC-10 above the purity
of a thick cloud ceiling in a vault of purest blue.
She feels safe.   Here, no one can reach her.
Neither men nor women have her in their power.

Because I have sometimes been her, because I am of her,
I watch her with eyes that blink away like a flash
cruelly, when she does what I don't want to see.
I am tired of innocence and its uselessness,
sometimes the dream of innocence beguiles me.
Nothing has told me how to think of her power.

Blurredly, apple-blossom drifts
across rough earth, small trees contort and twist
making their own shapes, wild.   Why should we love purity?
Can the woman in the DC-10 see this
and would she call this innocence?   If no one can reach her
she is drawing on unnamed, unaccountable power.

This woman I have been and recognize
must know that beneath the quilt of whiteness lies
a hated nation, hers,
earth whose wet places call to mind
still-open wounds:    her country.
Do we love purity?   Where do we turn for power?

Knowing us as I do I cringe when she says
*But I was not culpable,*
*I was the victim, the girl, the youngest,*
*the susceptible one, I was sick,*
*the one who simply had to get out, and did*
: I am still trying how to think of her power.

And if she was forced, this woman, by the same
white Dixie boy who took for granted as prey
her ignored dark sisters?     What if at five years old
she was old to his fingers splaying her vulva open
what if forever after, in every record
she wants her name inscribed as *innocent*

and will not speak, refuses to know, can say
*I have been numb for years*
does not want to hear of any violation
like or unlike her own, as if the victim
can be innocent only in isolation
as if the victim dare not be intelligent

*(I have been numb for years):* and if this woman
longs for an intact world, an intact soul,
longs for what we all long for, yet denies us all?
What has she smelled of power without once
tasting it in the mouth?  For what protections
has she traded her wildness and the lives of others?

There is a porch in Salem, Virginia
that I have never seen, that may no longer stand,
honeysuckle vines twisting above the talk,

a driveway full of wheeltracks, paths going down
to the orchards, apple and peach,
divisions so deep a wild child lost her way.

A child climbing an apple-tree in Virginia
refuses to come down, at last comes down
for a neighbour's lying bribe.   Now, if that child, grown old
feels safe in a DC-10 above thick white clouds
and no one can reach her
and if that woman's child, another woman

chooses another way, yet finds the old vines
twisting across her path, the old wheeltracks
how does she stop dreaming the dream
of protection, how does she follow her own wildness
shedding the innocence, the childish power?
How does she keep from dreaming the old dreams?

*1983*

## POETRY: I

Someone at a table under a brown metal lamp
is studying the history of poetry.
Someone in the library at closing-time
has learned to say *modernism,*
*trope, vatic, text.*
She is listening for shreds of music.
He is searching for his name
back in the old country.
They cannot learn without teachers.
They are like us     what we were
if you remember.

In a corner of night a voice
is crying in a kind of whisper:
*More!*

Can you remember?     when we thought
the poets taught     how to live?
That is not the voice of a critic
nor a common reader
it is someone young     in anger
hardly knowing what to ask
who finds our lines     our glosses
wanting     in this world.

*1985*

# POETRY: II, CHICAGO

Whatever a poet is
at the point of conception     is
conceived in these projects
of beige and grey bricks     Yes, poets are born
in wasted tracts like these     whatever colour, sex
comes to term in this winter's driving nights
And the child pushes like a spear
a cry     through cracked cement     through zero air
a spear, a cry of green     Yes, poets endure
these schools of fear     balked yet unbroken
where so much gets broken:  trust
windows   pride     the mothertongue

Wherever a poet is born     enduring
depends on the frailest of chances:
Who listened to your murmuring
over your little rubbish     who let you be
who gave you the books
who let you know you were not
alone     showed you the twist
of old strands     raffia, hemp or silk
the beaded threads     the fiery lines
saying:  *This belongs to you     you have the right*
*you belong to the song*
*of your mothers and fathers     You have a people*

*1984*

129

# POETRY: III

Even if we knew the children were all asleep
and healthy    the ledgers balanced    the water running
clear in the pipes
                            and all the prisoners free

Even if every word we wrote by then
were honest    the sheer heft
of our living behind it
                            not these sometimes
lax, indolent lines
                    these litanies

Even if we were told    not just by friends
that this was honest work

Even if each of us didn't wear
a brass locket with a picture
of a strangled woman    a girlchild sewn through the crotch

Even if someone had told us, young: *This is not a key*
*nor a peacock feather*
                    *not a kite nor a telephone*
*This is the kitchen sink    the grinding-stone*

would we give ourselves
more calmly over    feel less criminal joy
when the thing comes    as it does come
clarifying grammar
and the fixed and mutable stars – ?

*1984*

*from*

*TIME'S POWER*

*(1989)*

# CHILDREN PLAYING CHECKERS
# AT THE EDGE OF THE FOREST

Two green-webbed chairs

                              a three-legged stool between

Your tripod

              Spears of grass

                          longer than your bare legs

cast shadows on your legs

                    drawn up

                          from the red-and-black

cardboard squares

                   the board of play

                        the board of rules

But you're not playing, you're talking

                       It's midsummer

and greater rules are breaking

                 It's the last

innocent summer you will know

                   and I

will go on awhile pretending that's not true

When I have done pretending

                  I can see this:

the depth of the background

               shadows

                         not of one moment only

erased and charcoaled in again

                  year after year

how the tree looms back behind you
the first tree of the forest

                the last tree

from which the deer step out

                   from protection

                              the first tree

into dreadfulness

            The last and the first tree

*1987*

# SLEEPWALKING    NEXT TO DEATH

*Sleep    horns of a snail*
                        protruding, retracting
What we choose to know
                    or not know
                                all these years
*sleepwalking*
            *next to death*

*I*

This snail could have been eaten
This snail could have been crushed
This snail could have dreamed it was a painter or a poet
This snail could have driven fast at night
putting up graffiti with a spray-gun:

This snail could have ridden
in the back of the pick-up, handing guns

*II*

Knows, chooses not to know
                        It has always
been about death and chances
                    The Dutch artist wrote and painted
one or more strange and usable things
For I mean to meet you
in any land    in any language

This is my promise:
I will be there
if you are there

*III*

In between this and that there are different places
of waiting, airports mostly where the air
is hungover, visibility low     boarding passes not guaranteed
If you wrote me, *I sat next to Naomi*
I would read that, *someone who felt like Ruth*
I would begin reading you like a dream
That's how extreme it feels

                            that's what I have to do

*IV*

Every stone around your neck you know the reason for
at this time in your life     Relentlessly
you tell me their names and furiously I
forget their names     Forgetting the names of the stones
you love, you lover of stones
what is it I do?

*V*

What is it I do?  I refuse to take your place
in the world     I refuse to make myself
your courier     I refuse so much
I might ask, what is it I do?
I will not be the dreamer for whom

you are the only dream
I will not be your channel
I will wrestle you to the end
for our difference (as you have wrestled me)
I will change your name and confuse
the Angel

*VI*

I am stupid with you and practical with you
I remind you to take a poultice    forget a quarrel
I am a snail in the back of the pick-up handing you
vitamins you hate to take

*VII*

Calmly you look over my shoulder    at this page    and say
*It's all about you    None of this*
*tells my story*

*VIII*

Yesterday noon I stood by a river
and many waited to cross over
from the Juarez barrio

                              to El Paso del Norte
First day of spring    a stand of trees
in Mexico were in palegreen leaf
a man casting a net

                      into the Rio Grande
and women, in pairs, strolling

                              across the border
as if taking a simple walk
                        Many thousands go


I stood by the river and thought of you
young    in Mexico    in a time of hope


*IX*


The practical nurse is the only nurse
with her plastic valise of poultices and salves
her hands of glove leather and ebony
her ledgers of pain
The practical nurse goes down to the river
in her runover shoes and her dollar necklace
eating a burrito in hand
                        it will be a long day
a long labour
                the midwife will be glad to see her
it will be a long night    someone bleeding
from a botched abortion    a beating    Will you let her
            touch you now?
Will you tell her you're fine?


*X*


I'm afraid of the border patrol
                        Not those men
of La Migra who could have run us
into the irrigation canal with their van
                              I'm afraid

of the patrollers
the sleepwalker in me

          the loner in you

*XI*

I want five hours with you
in a train running south

                maybe ten hours
in a Greyhound bound for the border
the two seats side-by-side that become a home
an island of light in the continental dark
the time that takes the place of a lifetime
I promise I won't fall asleep when the lights go down
I will not be lulled
Promise you won't jump the train
vanish into the bus depot at three a.m.
that you won't defect

              that we'll travel
like two snails

         our four horns erect

*1987*

# DELTA

If you have taken this rubble for my past
raking through it for fragments you could sell
know that I long ago moved on
deeper into the heart of the matter

If you think you can grasp me, think again:
my story flows in more than one direction
a delta springing from the riverbed
with its five fingers spread


*1987*

# DREAMWOOD

In the old, scratched, cheap wood of the typing stand
there is a landscape, veined, which only a child can see
or the child's older self,
a woman dreaming when she should be typing
the last report of the day.   If this were a map,
she thinks, a map laid down to memorize
because she might be walking it, it shows
ridge upon ridge fading into hazed desert,
here and there a sign of aquifers
and one possible watering-hole.   If this were a map
it would be the map of the last age of her life,
not a map of choices but a map of variations
on the one great choice.   It would be the map by which
she could see the end of touristic choices,
of distances blued and purpled by romance,
by which she would recognize that poetry
isn't revolution but a way of knowing
why it must come.   If this cheap, massproduced
wooden stand from the Brooklyn Union Gas Co.,
massproduced yet durable, being here now,
is what it is yet a dream-map
so obdurate, so plain,
she thinks, the material and the dream can join
and that is the poem and that is the late report.

*1987*

# DIVISIONS OF LABOUR

The revolutions wheel, compromise, utter their statements:
a new magazine appears, mastheaded with old names,
an old magazine polishes up its act
with deconstructions of the prose of Malcolm X
The women in the back rows of politics
are still licking thread to slip into the needle's
eye, trading bones for plastic, splitting pods
for necklaces to sell to the cruise-ships
producing immaculate First Communion dresses
with flatiron and irresolute hot water
still fitting the microscopic golden wires
into the silicon chips
still teaching, watching the children
quenched in the crossfire alleys, the flashflood gullies
the kerosene flashfires
— the women whose labour remakes the world
each and every morning
                          I have seen a woman sitting
between the stove and the stars
her fingers singed from snuffing out the candles
of pure theory    Finger and thumb: both scorched:
I have felt that sacred wax blister my hand

*1988*

*from*

## AN ATLAS OF THE

## DIFFICULT WORLD

*(1991)*

## *from* AN ATLAS OF THE DIFFICULT WORLD

*I*

A dark woman, head bent, listening for something
– a woman's voice, a man's voice or
voice of the freeway, night after night, metal streaming
        downcoast
past eucalyptus, cypress, agribusiness empires
THE SALAD BOWL OF THE WORLD, gurr of small planes
dusting the strawberries, each berry picked by a hand
in close communion, strawberry blood on the wrist,
Malathion in the throat, communion,
the hospital at the edge of the fields,
prematures slipping from unsafe wombs,
the labour and delivery nurse on her break watching
planes dusting rows of pickers.
Elsewhere declarations are made:  at the sink
rinsing strawberries flocked and gleaming, fresh from market
one says: 'On the pond this evening is a light
finer than my mother's handkerchief
received from her mother, hemmed and initialled
by the nuns in Belgium.'
One says: 'I can lie for hours
reading and listening to music.  But sleep comes hard.
I'd rather lie awake and read.'  One writes:
'Mosquitoes pour through the cracks
in this cabin's walls, the road
in winter is often impassable,
I live here so I don't have to go out and act,

I'm trying to hold onto my life, it feels like nothing.'
One says: 'I never knew from one day to the next
where it was coming from:  I had to make my life happen
from day to day.  Every day an emergency.
Now I have a house, a job from year to year.
What does that make me?'
In the writing workshop a young man's tears
wet the frugal beard he's grown to go with his poems
hoping they have redemption stored
in their lines, maybe will get him home free.  In the classroom
eight-year-old faces are grey.  The teacher knows which
        children
have not broken fast that day,
remembers the Black Panthers spooning cereal.


∞ ∞ ∞


I don't want to hear how he beat her after the earthquake,
tore up her writing, threw the kerosene
lantern into her face waiting
like an unbearable mirror of his own.  I don't
want to hear how she finally ran from the trailer
how he tore the keys from her hands, jumped into the truck
and backed it into her. I don't want to think
how her guesses betrayed her – that he meant well, that she
was really the stronger and ought not to leave him
to his own apparent devastation.  I don't want to know
wreckage, dreck and waste, but these are the materials
and so are the slow lift of the moon's belly
over wreckage, dreck, and waste, wild treefrogs calling in
another season, light and music still pouring over
our fissured, cracked terrain.

∞ ∞ ∞

Within two miles of the Pacific rounding
this long bay, sheening the light for miles
inland, floating its fog through redwood rifts and over
strawberry and artichoke fields, its bottomless mind
returning always to the same rocks, the same cliffs, with
ever-changing words, always the same language
 – this is where I live now.   If you had known me
once, you'd still know me now though in a different
light and life.   This is no place you ever knew me.


But it would not surprise you
to find me here, walking in fog, the sweep of the great ocean
eluding me, even the curve of the bay, because as always
I fix on the land.   I am stuck to earth.   What I love here
is old ranches, leaning seaward, lowroofed spreads
            between rocks
small canyons running through pitched hillsides
liveoaks twisted on steepness, the eucalyptus avenue
            leading
to the wrecked homestead, the fogwreathed heavy-
            chested cattle
on their blond hills.   I drive inland over roads
closed in wet weather, past shacks hunched in the canyons
roads that crawl down into darkness and wind into light
where trucks have crashed and riders of horses tangled
to death with lowstruck boughs.   These are not the roads
you knew me by.   But the woman driving, walking,
            watching
for life and death, is the same.

*II*

Here is a map of our country:
here is the Sea of Indifference, glazed with salt
This is the haunted river flowing from brow to groin
we dare not taste its water
This is the desert where missiles are planted like corms
This is the breadbasket of foreclosed farms
This is the birthplace of the rockabilly boy
This is the cemetery of the poor
who died for democracy     This is a battlefield
from a nineteenth-century war     the shrine is famous
This is the sea-town of myth and story     when the
          fishing fleets
went bankrupt     here is where the jobs were     on the pier
processing frozen fishsticks     hourly wages and no shares
These are other battlefields     Centralia     Detroit
here are the forests primeval     the copper     the silver lodes
These are the suburbs of acquiescence     silence rising
          fumelike from the streets
This is the capital of money and dolour whose spires
flare up through air inversions whose bridges are crumbling
whose children are drifting blind alleys pent
between coiled rolls of razor wire
I promised to show you a map you say but this is a mural
then yes let it be     these are small distinctions
where do we see it from is the question

148

*IV*

Late summers, early autumns, you can see something
   that binds
the map of this country together:   the girasol, orange
   gold-petalled
with her black eye, laces the roadsides from Vermont
   to California
runs the edges of orchards, chain-link fences
milo fields and malls, schoolyards and reservations
truckstops and quarries, grazing ranges, graveyards
of veterans, graveyards of cars hulked and sunk, her
   tubers the jerusalem artichoke
that has fed the Indians, fed the hobos, could feed us all.
Is there anything in the soil, cross-country, that makes for
a plant so generous?   *Spendthrift* we say, as if
accounting nature's waste.   Ours darkens
the states to their strict borders, flushes
down borderless streams, leaches from lakes to the
   curdled foam
down by the riverside.

Waste.   Waste.   The watcher's eye put out, hands of the
   builder severed, brain of the maker starved
those who could bind, join, reweave, cohere, replenish
now at risk in this segregate republic
locked away out of sight and hearing, out of mind,
   shunted aside
those needed to teach, advise, persuade, weigh arguments
those urgently needed for the work of perception
work of the poet, the astronomer, the historian, the
   architect of new streets

work of the speaker who also listens
meticulous delicate work of reaching the heart of the
            desperate woman, the desperate man
– never-to-be-finished, still unbegun work of repair –
            it cannot be done without them
and where are they now?


*VIII*


He thought there would be a limit and that it would stop
            him. He depended on that:
the cuts would be made by someone else, the direction
come from somewhere else, arrows flashing on the freeway.
That he'd end somewhere gazing
straight into It was what he imagined and nothing beyond.
That he'd end facing as limit a thing without limits and
            so he flung
and burned and hacked and bled himself toward that (if I
            understand
this story at all). What he found: FOR SALE: DO NOT
            DISTURB
OCCUPANT on some cliffs;   some ill-marked, ill-kept roads
ending in warnings about shellfish in Vietnamese,
            Spanish and English.
But the spray was any colour he could have dreamed
– gold, ash, azure, smoke, moonstone –
and from time to time the ocean swirled up through the
            eye of a rock and taught him
limits. Throwing itself backward, singing and sucking,
            no teacher, only its violent

self, the Pacific, dialectical waters rearing
their wild calm constructs, momentary, ancient.

∞ ∞ ∞

If your voice could overwhelm those waters, what would
          it say?
What would it cry of the child swept under, the mother
on the beach then, in her black bathing suit, walking
          straight out
into the glazed lace as if she never noticed, what would it
          say of the father
facing inland in his shoes and socks at the edge of the tide,
what of the lost necklace glittering twisted in foam?
If your voice could crack in the wind hold its breath still
          as the rocks
what would it say to the daughter searching the tidelines
          for a bottled message
from the sunken slaveships?   what of the huge sun
          slowly defaulting into the clouds
what of the picnic stored in the dunes at high tide, full of
          the moon, the basket
with sandwiches, eggs, paper napkins, can-opener, the meal
packed for a family feast, excavated now by scuttling
ants, sandcrabs, dune-rats, because no one understood
all picnics are eaten on the grave?

## XIII (Dedications)

I know you are reading this poem
late, before leaving your office
of the one intense yellow lamp-spot and the darkening
        window
in the lassitude of a building faded to quiet
long after rush-hour.  I know you are reading this poem
standing up in a bookstore far from the ocean
on a grey day of early spring, faint flakes driven
across the plains' enormous spaces around you.
I know you are reading this poem
in a room where too much has happened for you to bear
where the bedclothes lie in stagnant coils on the bed
and the open valise speaks of flight
but you cannot leave yet. I know you are reading this poem
as the underground train loses momentum and before
        running up the stairs
toward a new kind of love
your life has never allowed.
I know you are reading this poem by the light
of the television screen where soundless images jerk and slide
while you wait for the newscast from the *intifada*.
I know you are reading this poem in a waiting-room
of eyes met and unmeeting, of identity with strangers.
I know you are reading this poem by fluorescent light
in the boredom and fatigue of the young who are counted out,
count themselves out, at too early an age.  I know
you are reading this poem through your failing sight, the thick
lens enlarging these letters beyond all meaning yet you
        read on

because even the alphabet is precious.
I know you are reading this poem as you pace beside the stove
warming milk, a crying child on your shoulder, a book in
　　　your hand
because life is short and you too are thirsty.
I know you are reading this poem which is not in your
　　　language
guessing at some words while others keep you reading
and I want to know which words they are.
I know you are reading this poem listening for something,
　　　torn between bitterness and hope
turning back once again to the task you cannot refuse.
I know you are reading this poem because there is nothing
　　　else left to read
there where you have landed, stripped as you are.


*1990-1991*

# MARGHANITA

at the oak table under the ceiling fan
Marghanita at the table counting up
a dead woman's debts.
Kicks off a sandal, sips
soda from a can, wedges the last bills
under the candelabrum.   She is here
because no one else was there when worn-to-skeleton
her enemy died.   Her love.   Her twin.
Marghanita dreamed the intravenous, the intensive
the stainless steel
before she ever saw them.   She's not practical,
you know, they used to say.
She's the artist, she got away.

In her own place Marghanita glues bronze
feathers into wings, smashes green and clear
bottles into bloodletting particles
crushed into templates of sand
scores mirrors till they fall apart and sticks them up
in driftwood boughs, drinks golden
liquid with a worm's name, forgets
her main enemy, her twin;
scores her wrist on a birthday
dreams the hospital dream.

When they were girl and  boy together, boy and girl
she pinned his arm against his back
for a box containing false

lashes and fingernails, a set of veils, a string of pearls,
she let go and listened to his tales
she breathed their breath, he hers,
they each had names only the other knew.

Marghanita in the apartment everyone has left:
not a nephew, not a niece,
nobody from the parish
 – gone into hiding, emigrated, lost?
where are the others?
Marghanita comes back because she does,
adding up what's left:
a rainsoaked chequebook, snapshots
razed from an album,
colours ground into powder, brushes, wands
for eyelids, lashes, brows,
beads of bath-oil, tubes of glycerin
 – a dead woman's luxuries.

Marghanita will
take care of it all.   Pay if nothing else
the last month's rent.   The wings of the fan
stir corners of loose paper,
light ebbs from the window-lace,
she needs to go out and eat.   And so
hating and loving come down
to a few columns of figures,
an aching stomach, a care taken:   something done.

*1989*

# FINAL NOTATIONS

it will not be simple, it will not be long
it will take little time, it will take all your thought
it will take all your heart, it will take all your breath
it will be short, it will not be simple

it will touch through your ribs, it will take all your heart
it will not be long, it will occupy your thought
as a city is occupied, as a bed is occupied
it will take all your flesh, it will not be simple

You are coming into us who cannot withstand you
you are coming into us who never wanted to withstand you
you are taking parts of us into places never planned
you are going far away with pieces of our lives

it will be short, it will take all your breath
it will not be simple, it will become your will

1991

*from*

*DARK FIELDS OF THE REPUBLIC*

*Poems 1991 - 1995*

(1995)

# SIX NARRATIVES

*1*

You drew up the story of your life    I was in that story
Nights on the coast I'd meet you flashlight in hand
curving my soles over musseled rocks    cracked and raw
            we'd lick inside the shells for danger
You'd drop into the bar    I'd sit upstairs at my desk
            writing the pages
you hoped would make us famous    then in the face of
            my turned back
you went to teach at the freedom school as if
you were teaching someone else to get free from me
            this was your story
Like a fogsmeared planet over the coast
I'd walked into, served, your purposeful longings
            I knew, I did not stop    till I turned my back

2

You drew up a story about me    I fled that story
Aching in mind I noticed names on the helms of busses:
        COP CITY    SHEEPSHEAD BAY
I thought I saw the city where the cops came home
to lay kitchen linoleum    barbecue on balconies
I saw the bloodied head of the great sheep dragged
        through the underpasses
trucked to the bay where the waters would not touch it
left on the beach in its shroud of flies
On the bus to La Guardia my arms ached with all
        my findings
anchored under my breasts with all my will
I cried *sick day, O sick day, this is my day and I, for this*
        *I will not pay*
as the green rushed bleeding out through the snarled
        cracks of the expressway

*3*

You were telling a story about women to young men
        It was not my story
it was not a story about women it was a story about men
Your hunger a spear gripped in hand a tale unspun in
        your rented campground
clothed in captured whale-songs tracked with
        synthesized Andes flutes
it was all about you    beaded and bearded
        misfeathered and miscloaked
where the TV cameras found you in your sadness

4

You were telling a story about love    it was your story
I came and stood outside
listening :    : death was in the doorway
death was in the air but the story
had its own life    no pretenses
about women in that lovesong for a man
Listening I went inside the bow scraping the bass-string
inside the horn's heartbroken cry
I was the breath's intake the bow's rough mutter:
*Vigil for boy of responding kisses, (never again on earth responding,)*
*Vigil for comrade swiftly slain . . .*

*5*

I was telling you a story about love
how even in war it goes on speaking its own language

Yes you said but the larynx is bloodied
the knife was well-aimed into the throat

Well I said love is hated     it has no price

No you said     you are talking about feelings
Have you ever felt nothing?     that is what war is now

Then a shadow skimmed your face
Go on talking in a normal voice     you murmured
Nothing is listening

*6*

You were telling a story about war     it is our story
an old story     and still it must be told
the story of the new that fled the old
how the big dream strained and shifted
the ship of hope shuddered on the iceberg's breast
the private affections swayed and staggered
So we are thrown together     so we are racked apart
in a republic shivering on     its glassy lips
parted     as if the fundamental rift
had not been calculated from the first into the mighty
          scaffold.


*1994*

## An Afterword

I first heard Adrienne Rich's name on the sidewalk of Garden Street, in Cambridge, Massachusetts, in the fall of 1952 – I was a freshman at Radcliffe College (the women's part of Harvard), and Adrienne had just graduated from there the year before. She had published her first book, *A Change of World*, while she was an undergraduate; her book was chosen for The Yale Series of Younger Poets by Auden, who said her poems were 'neatly and modestly dressed.' When she wanted to read a book or listen to a tape (in those days, a record) in The Woodberry Poetry Room at Harvard, Jack Sweeney, the librarian, had to meet her outside Lamont Library and escort her in – women were not allowed.

Walking down the sidewalk of Garden Street that September, I met an old gentleman, very courteous; he asked me what I wanted to study at college, and I said I wanted to write poetry. And he said, 'We're very proud here, you know, of Adrienne Rich. Have you read her book?' So I did, and I've been reading it ever since, the poems of Adrienne Rich, now launched in Dublin.

The way we met was characteristic of Adrienne: she got my first book of poetry, and read it, and wrote to me with the kind of encouragement only she could give. She was the first woman poet I had ever met. Later, in the sixties and early seventies, we were next-door neighbours in New York, and in that time of tumult and of hope, Adrienne and her family and I and my family were close companions. I remember when we first met, and she first met my oldest daughter, Sarah, who was ten, Adrienne said how beautiful she was, and how she felt as if she'd known her before. The quality of Adrienne's attention was enlarging, like the magnifying glass on the cover of one of her books.

We had a TV and they didn't, so I had the honour of getting to know Adrienne and Alf's two younger sons, Pablo and Jacob, watching a late afternoon serial called *Lost in Space*, for years and years and years. (Their older brother, David, was too old for such things.) And Adrienne and I showed each other our poems. We had lots of meals together in those days, but those readings of each other's poems were my meat and drink. She had, she has, the gift of letting you feel understood. – But those were hard years, too; and one of the joys of our long friendship is seeing each other happy now.

Her significance as a poet and feminist is legendary. She is for me a figure of integration: of life and art, of her own experience and experience beyond her own. She has asked a lot of her talent, and there has turned out to be very little her talent couldn't bear. Over the years her work has fulfilled Simone Weil's definition of love: 'The love of your neighbour in all its fullness simply means being able to say to him: What are you going through?'

In May of 1994 Adrienne visited Ireland, and read her work and met with Irish writers in Dublin and in the West, and even in such a short few days she fell in love with this quiet, beautiful, rainy country. She loved many things about it, but the thing I remember best is how she loved going through all the gates – the farm gates at the top and the bottom of our lane, the gate on the road up to

Carrowkeel – how it slows you down.

Nuala Ní Dhomhnaill has written about the Irish-speaking people coming to the English language as a mermaid coming to live on the land. The mermaid wakes up in the hospital and there's a nurse explaining what her legs are for, and how to use them.

Women are not new to poetry, but only to translating it into the language of the upper air. Now we are here with our legs under us, and Adrienne one of the surest and earthiest among us; but we've kept our tails, too, and Adrienne, as she was in the beginning, is still our brilliant sculler.


*Jean Valentine*
Sligo 1995